Sojourn

A Woman's Guide to Camping Alone

Laura Stockwell

© 2018 by Laura Stockwell
First Edition
ISBN 978-0-692-14293-6
Edited by Charles Stockwell
Illustrations by Laura Stockwell
Printed in USA

Dedicated to those
who put the wild in my heart
and perhaps even more to those
who never sought to tame it.

Contents

Introduction

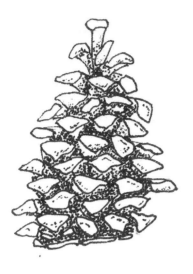

Camping alone. Sound intimidating?

You enjoy hiking alone in the woods or along the beach. You enjoy spending quiet time outdoors, watching the clouds, listening to the water. What if you didn't have to drive home at the end of the day? What if you could just head back to your campsite, build a crackling fire, fall to sleep in a cozy sleeping bag, wake up at dawn, and do it all over again? If you've sometimes thought about doing this, but aren't quite sure how to get started, then this is the book for you.

There are three main ways to go camping alone: *backpacking, car-camping in a camper,* and *car-camping in a tent.*

Backpacking means loading your stuff into a backpack and carrying it on foot to a campsite. Backpacking alone can

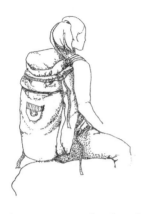

be risky. Generally you hike for many miles to a remote location. If you've forgotten something, you'll either have to walk all the way back to get it or do without. If you cut yourself or break your ankle, you'll have to get back to your vehicle somehow and drive yourself to a medical facility. Furthermore, backpacking gear is expensive. Since you carry everything on your back, it has to be lightweight. Recently I priced the ultra light gear I would need for a backpacking trip, and it came to more than $1,000. If you're just starting out, I don't recommend backpacking alone.

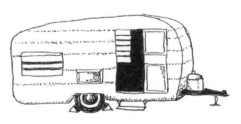

Car-camping in a camper means bringing a little house-on-wheels with you to the campsite. Campers come in all sizes, from tiny pop-ups that you can tow behind your Prius to luxury behemoths that you must tow behind a Ford F350 Super Duty. In addition, there are self-propelled motor homes (also called Recreational Vehicles or RVs). Camping in a camper (or motor home) certainly is a convenient way to go, but it isn't really camping. Besides, campers are expensive and the price of a motor home will take your breath away. I don't recommend car-camping in a camper.

Car-camping in a tent means driving to a campsite and pitching a tent with your car parked either at the site or within easy walking distance— say, less than half a mile. You throw your stuff in the car, drive to the campsite, park, unload, set it up, and you're camping. This is the type of camping that I think is most suitable for women starting out to camp alone and for the most part, the type I'm going to talk about in this book.

One more thing. As women, we are not expected to take time away from the hustle and bustle of daily life. We're expected to be givers, to take care of others, and to look good while doing it. As women, we're not expected to be self-reliant, we're not expected to travel alone, or sleep in tents, or build fires, or go into the wild without men by our sides. But there's no reason why we can't do these things. No reason at all. I'm proposing that we spend some time by ourselves without phones to answer, dishes to wash, emails to respond to, children to ferry, laundry to fold, or meals to prepare. Time spent learning that we can do whatever we decide to do. Time spent enjoying the present. End of sermon.

■ ■
■ ■

I grew up in a Detroit suburb. In all of my childhood years, I never went camping. Not once. When I was seven years old, I did travel with my family to Washington State and stayed in a cabin beside the Hoh River and that left a solid impression on me. But I never camped. I've always liked being outdoors and played outside all the time, but I never spent time in the woods. I was a city kid, through and through. I could navigate highways and byways and I had some street smarts. But I never learned to read a map or pitch a tent.

When I was sixteen years old, I camped for the first time in Caseville, Michigan, with some friends. I have to say, I was stunned. We camped in a scrubby little patch of second-growth forest, all bracken ferns and skinny poplar trees, but I was sure I was in the wilderness. I imagined bears, saw birds I'd only seen in books, and was thrilled by the sight of a white-tailed deer. I camped a few times after that during my high school years, always with other people, usually in civilized campgrounds. I left the Detroit area and went to college in a small rural town. During my first year, I was so homesick for the five-lane highways and fast-paced city that I went home every weekend. I referred to the locals in disparaging terms and hated all things rural. I despised farm fields, snowy back roads, and mosquitoes. I never left the little college town except to drive home.

After a year or so in college, I got a job that required travelling to rural areas. I found that I enjoyed the drive and the scenery. I also went fishing in the local park and I caught fish. So I started exploring and fishing in the local river and found myself outside and really enjoying the time away from town and the quietness of the outdoors. There was also a forest (more mature than the scrubby one of my first camping experience) surrounding the river in that little town. I found a lot of peace in that canopied space. I took to studying in the park, fishing in the early morning after a midnight shift, and learning to read a map to see where else I could go fishing.

I took a biology class in college and the professor insisted we know the name of every bird, mammal, tree, and most shrubs in the State of Michigan. For the final exam, he placed taxidermy animals and preserved leaves on the lab tables and we had to go through all of them and write down what they were. Did you know there are 365 species of birds in the State of Michigan?

I was thrilled with that class because all of a sudden the trees and types of forests and frogs had names. I was so thrilled I started reading and studying ecosystems and animals on my own. I'd always been interested in the outdoors, but I reached a new level of fervor after that class. After I graduated, I ended up becoming a nature center camp counselor in a nearby town during the summers.

I camped a few times as an adult, but was pretty much consumed with marriage, school, and work. Then there was graduation, so no more school, and then there was divorce, so no more marriage. I came out of a ten-year marriage with no hobbies of my own. I felt lost, unable to function without someone to take care of. The only thing I knew was that I loved being outdoors.

I spent time on day trips exploring trails and rivers. I hiked the local city forest in the little town I moved to. I drove an hour or so to hike a larger county park on weekends. I spent a lot of time outdoors when I wasn't working, but I knew I wanted to spend even more time in wilderness areas. Days perhaps.

So I made a bold declaration to my friends: I was going camping. By myself. I'm sure they thought I was crazy. I went to the store, bought a tent, and drove. I had a vague destination in mind, but nothing really solid. I knew how to read a map, so I tossed a little street map into the car along with my new tent, a borrowed sleeping bag, and about $60 in my purse and started driving north and west.

Since then, I've gone camping alone whenever I had a chance. I've made mistakes, gotten hurt a time or two, and once met a bear. I've spent countless hours on back roads, pitching tents, waiting out rainstorms, and watching the sun set over Lake Michigan. I've learned a lot. Now I'm going to share it. I hope that by giving you some basic information about how to get started and telling you a small story or two, I can convince you to try camping alone yourself.

■ ■
■ ■

Choosing a Campsite

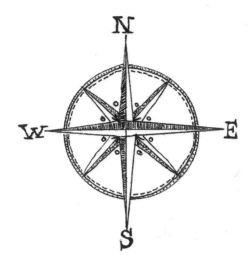

Where do you want to camp? Wide open spaces? The beach? A deep dark forest? A place where you remember camping as a child?

Go to the bookstore and buy a book of maps. More specifically, buy an "Atlas and Gazetteer" of your state (or the state you wish to camp in). You can buy road maps at gas stations and bookstores, but what you really want is a whole book of maps with the word, "Gazetteer," in the title. A Gazetteer gives you not only a road map, but also shows elevations, hills, forested areas, towns and cities, waterways, and points of interest. My favorite publisher is DeLorme. They publish an Atlas and Gazetteer for every state in the U.S. Inside one of their books, you will find highlighted campgrounds (public and private), waterways, state lands, and recreational areas.

Let's say you want to camp beside a stream. Then look at the key in the front of the map book and find the little icon that means campground (usually a picture of a tent). Now look along streams in your desired camping area and find one that has the little campground icon. That's where you camp. Interested in camping in hilly country? Look at the elevation lines. They designate changes in the height of the land. When the lines are far apart, the land is flat; when they are close together, you're in hilly country. If you want to camp in the woods, look for areas that are shaded green, especially those designated "State Forest" or "National Forest."

You ask, "Why not rely on internet maps?" Bad idea. What if you're out in the woods and your internet doesn't work? You really need to buy an Atlas and Gazetteer for the state you plan to camp in, learn how to read it, and carry it with you in your car.

Not sure how to read a map? The top of the page is north, the bottom is south, the right side is east, and the left side is west. Start learning to read a map by opening the map book to the page showing the neighborhood where you live. Find your house, find your local grocery store, and trace the route between the two. You already know the route, so it shouldn't be hard. Continue to practice by finding other places on the map that you are already familiar with.

Now it's time to search the internet. Look for campgrounds on the web sites of your state's Bureau of Land Management (BLM), Department of Natural Resources (DNR), Fish and Wildlife Department, and the U.S. Forest Service. There are many campgrounds run by government agencies in which you can camp for $15 to $25 per night. There are private campgrounds too, but usually they are busier and cost more.

When you're first starting out, camp only in designated campgrounds. You need a special permit to camp anywhere else on public land and if you don't have one, a conservation officer probably will pay you a visit and in my experience, she will do so at first light. Never camp on private land without the land owner's permission. That's trespassing. Try to find a campground that is plain and simple. Many campgrounds offer amenities like mini-golf courses, electrical outlets, flushing toilets, and hot showers, but along with these amenities usually come neighboring campers who are too close and too loud. A campground with lots of amenities may be suitable for families with kids, but not for a woman seeking solitude.

∷

I'll admit it. The first time I went camping alone, I just started driving with no real idea of where I was headed. I didn't consult a map. I drove north and west until I spotted a brown "State Campground" sign, turned off the main road, followed a two-track for a couple miles, and found myself at a quiet campground beside a blue ribbon trout stream. So it turned out all right.

When I got home, I bought myself a DeLorme Atlas and Gazetteer. Years later, I still have it. I've spent many evenings poring over its many pages, tracing small squiggly lines across the maps, looking for the most interesting back roads and remote campsites. I've balanced that map on the car console next to me while bouncing down two-tracks and I've made notes on most of the pages about conditions of campgrounds and roads. I've taped pages back together after they have been torn off in the car door. The pages are wrinkled and bumpy and coffee-stained from being opened and closed countless times on damp campground picnic tables. Page 96 is pretty much one big coffee stain and my notes on that page are now meaningless pencil smudges. I know that the two-track road on page 76 washed out in 2005 and someday I'll get back there to see if it's been repaired. There's a campground on page 89 that I drove through once, but have never camped at. I'll check it out next time I'm in the area. The paper is soft, almost like fabric. It's moldy from a season spent in the car after being rained upon and smells decidedly campfire-y.

But I still have my DeLorme Atlas and Gazetteer and still use it. Every so often I just take it into my head to start driving and sometimes end up lost on a two-track deep in the woods without cell phone coverage. When that happens, I just pull over, reach into the back seat until my fingers settle on my well-worn and well-loved old map, and find out where I am.

. .
. .

Choosing a Tent

You'll need a tent. Sure, you could sleep in your car, but that's uncomfortable and it's not really camping. So go buy yourself a tent. They provide protection from rain and mosquitoes (and who knows what other critters) and they are great for stashing your stuff when you go hiking. A hanging hammock is another option and it might be all you need, but not where there are mosquitoes. You need serious protection from mosquitoes when you are sleeping. There's nothing better than lying quietly inside your tent and listening to noises at night. It might be a little scary when the coyotes start howling. (They won't come into your campsite—promise.) But you may also hear a great horned owl hooting under a full spring moon and spruce boughs sighing in a summer breeze off the lake.

There are many types of tents on the market, ranging from huge sidewall tents for the whole family to ultra light one-person tents for backpackers. The best tent for solo car camping is a two-person dome tent. If you want to spend a lot of money, you can buy a top-of-the-line dome tent at an outdoor store, such as REI—they cost about $400—but you can also buy an adequate tent for about $60 from Wal-Mart and that's what I recommend. Here's what you get:

(1) The tent itself with a zippered opening and sleeves (or clips) for attaching the tent poles.

(2) The rain fly, which covers the tent to provide a barrier from the rain.

(3) Two (sometimes three) tent poles, each comprised of about ten one-foot-long sections. Usually the sections are connected together with a bungee cord or other stretchy material, but for some tents, the pole sections are threaded at the ends and meant to be screwed together.

(4) Tent stakes to fix the tent to the ground. There should be between four and ten of them. The stakes that come with cheap tents are flimsy, so you may wish to buy a set of sturdier stakes separately. You will also need a small hammer to pound the stakes into hard ground.

(5) Some tents come with bungee cords to attach the rain fly to the tent poles or attach the tent to the stakes.

(6) Some tents come with a plastic tarp. If not, I recommend that you buy one separately. The tarp goes under the tent to provide a moisture barrier between the tent and the ground.

I highly recommend that you practice pitching your tent at home before you go camping. Here's how you do it:

(1) Fold the plastic tarp to about the size and shape of your tent. Don't worry about making it perfect, because you'll be able to tuck the edges under your tent after you put it up.

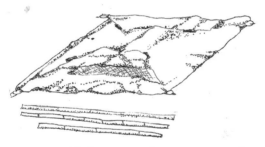

(2) Lay out all the parts of your tent on the tarp and inspect them to make sure everything is there and in good working condition.

(3) Connect the tent poles. Snap (or screw) the sections of the two (or three) poles together and lay them on the ground.

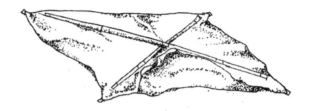

(4) Lay the tent out flat on the tarp and cross two of the tent poles over it where they'll eventually go to make sure you've got them in the right location. These two poles should form an "X" pattern across the tent and each pole should rest on one of the tent's sleeves (or clips). When you're sure they're positioned correctly, push each pole through its sleeve (or attach it to its clips). If your tent has three poles, the third one attaches to the sleeve (or clips) on the rain fly. Its purpose is to hold the rain fly away from the tent opening.

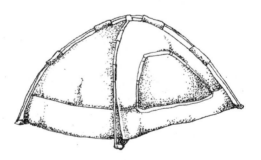

(5) Raise the tent by inserting the tips of the poles into the eyelets at the corners of the tent. The poles will bow upward, the fabric will stretch, and the tent will pop up. Voila!

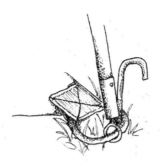

(6) Stake the tent to the ground. For most tents, there are little loops at each corner (and some-times also in the center of the sides). Push a stake through the first loop and drive it into the ground. Do the same with the remaining stakes, each time pulling the bottom of the tent outward so the floor becomes taut. For some tents, you first drive the stakes into the ground and then attach the corners of the tent to the stakes with bungee cords.

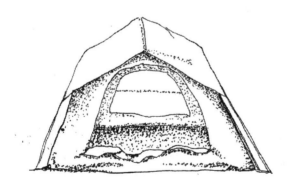

(7) If there's a third pole, push it through the sleeve (or clips) of the rain fly. Then position the

rain fly over the top of the tent with the pole (if any) over the tent opening. Fasten down the rain fly. For some tents, you fasten it to the tent poles with Velcro. For others, you fasten it to the tent stakes with bungee cords.

(8) After you've gotten the tent up, make any adjustments needed to straighten it up and smooth out wrinkles. Then push the edges of the tarp under the tent. If you leave any of the tarp sticking out, water will pool under the tent when it rains.

If you take good care of your tent, it will last a long time. First rule: Do not store your tent if it is wet. If you must pack it up wet, then unpack it and pitch it in the back yard when you get home and let it dry out thoroughly. Second rule: Don't leave your tent pitched in the sun for long periods of time. The sun will damage the UV protection and the water repellent properties. Setting it up in a sunny spot to camp for a weekend is fine, but don't leave it out in the sun in the back yard all summer long. Even with proper care, your tent will develop rips and leaking seams, so eventually you'll need to make repairs. Tent repair kits are available at any outdoor store. It's good idea to buy one and take it along when you go camping.

■ ■
■ ■

I bought my first tent on clearance at the outlet store for $30 in 2002 and I'm still using it. The first night I slept in that tent, I listened to the wind blow through hemlocks, staring at that blue nylon, trying to be brave, but feeling a little nervous. I lay there thinking I would never fall asleep. The closing of car doors in the campground, *the snapping of twigs, and later the hoots of a great horned owl kept me wide-eyed. But I was determined to stay though the night and did finally fall asleep. I woke up at dawn to birdsong, snug in my little blue nylon tent.*

Since then, I've awakened many times in the same way in the same tent. I have slept in that tent in rain, snow, and 90 degree heat. I've shared that tent with two dogs. I've sometimes thought about buying a new tent, but my trusty old blue Coleman tent of 16 years feels like a home and I can live in it for a week at a time with no problem. It does smell a little musty though, probably because I put it away wet one time. That smell never goes away.

I remember once I went camping with an inexperienced friend. We were car-camping at a remote campground in the Porcupine Mountains near Lake Superior. We arrived late and it was raining—not pouring down, but misty and wet. We had maybe an hour before dark. When it's rainy like that, it gets dark fast and I was eager to set up camp and register before it was fully dark. In order to register at this particular campsite, you had to go to the campground and pick out your site, then drive back fifteen miles to the ranger station to register.

So I unpacked our rain canopy—a big four-post tent with a nylon cover—and told my inexperienced friend to set it up so she could get out of the rain while I went back and registered. I was gone maybe half an hour. When I came back, the mist had turned into drizzle and the rain canopy was still lying on the ground. My friend was frustrated, wet, and feeling terrible. I was feeling terrible, too. A rain canopy is easy to set up, so I assumed she would know how to do it or at least be able to figure it out. But she couldn't. So she ended up sitting in the rain in the wilderness, no cell service, completely on her own. I learned a lesson: Before you go camping, make sure you know how to set up your tent.

∷

Choosing a Sleeping Bag

You'll need a sleeping bag. When you go shopping for one, here's what to look for:

(1) **Temperature rating.** This is the lowest temperature for which a bag is designed to keep you warm (and that's assuming you are wearing long underwear and using a sleeping pad under the bag). Sleeping bags are typically categorized as follows: Summer (+35 degrees F and higher), 3-season (+10 to +30 degrees F), and Winter (+10 degrees F and lower). In other words, when a bag is described as a "summer bag," it means that most users should remain comfortable if the nighttime temperature stays above +35 degrees F. Choose a sleeping bag with a temperature rating a bit lower than the lowest temperature you expect to encounter. If you're headed for near-freezing temperatures, then choose a 3-season bag instead of a summer bag. If temperatures remain

higher than expected, you can easily unzip the bag to get more air circulation.

(2) **Shape.** Sleeping bags come in three different shapes: rectangular, semi-rectangular (or "barrel-shaped"), and mummy. You should know that sleeping bags are designed to keep you warm by trapping and holding a layer of "dead" (non-circulating) air next to your body. Your body heat warms the dead air, and the bag forms a barrier between you and the colder outside air. The less air space there is to heat, the faster you warm up and the warmer you stay. Rectangular bags are the least efficient in warming this dead space, but they are the roomiest and most comfortable and so are probably the best choice for car camping. Barrel-shaped bags offer greater warmth and efficiency than rectangular bags and are also suitable for car camping. Mummy bags are tight-fitting in order to maximize warmth and reduce weight, so they are popular with backpackers, but you don't really need all this efficiency for car camping and some people can't get comfortable sleeping in them. Note that you can also buy sleeping bags specifically designed for women. When compared to a standard bag, they are shorter, narrower at the shoulders, wider at the hips, and have more insulation in the upper body and foot box.

(3) **Insulation.** It will be either synthetic (typically polyester) or goose down. Most car campers choose synthetic fill because it is inexpensive, quick-drying, non-allergenic, and insulates even if it gets wet. Goose down is more expensive, but

many backpackers prefer it anyway because it rolls up tighter.

(4) **Water repellency.** The outer shell is typically made of rip-stop nylon or polyester. In many synthetic-fill bags, the shell fabric is treated with a durable water repellent (DWR) finish. To check if the shell has had a DWR treatment, rub a wet cloth across the surface. If the water beads up, then it has DWR.

Some sleeping bags come with additional features, such as:

(1) **A built-in hood.** When cinched with a draw cord, the hood prevents heat from radiating away from your head. Some hoods include a pillow pocket that you can stuff with clothing to create a pillow. You can also purchase a camping pillow separately or simply bring your own pillow from home.

(2) **A stash pocket** where you can keep small items, such as a cell phone or glasses when you sleep.

(3) **A sleeping pad sleeve** underneath the bag into which you can fit a sleeping pad. No more rolling off in the middle of the night.

(4) **A stuff sack** into which you put your sleeping bag after you roll it up.

There are also a couple of sleeping bag accessories to consider:

(1) **A cotton storage sack.** You will prolong the life of your sleeping bag if you hang it in the garage or store it loosely in a storage sack—not rolled up tight in its stuff sack. This keeps the insulation from getting permanently compressed, which would reduce the bag's insulating properties.

(2) **A sleeping bag liner.** A soft liner inside your bag helps to keep it clean and minimize wear. It also adds an extra 8 to 15 degrees F of warmth, so you can sleep comfortably at lower temperatures. And when it's hot outside, you can skip the bag and just sleep in the liner.

You're going to want a sleeping pad under your bag. Sleeping pads play two important roles for getting a solid night's sleep—cushioning and insulation. It might seem like having a soft surface to sleep on is a pad's main function, but its ability to insulate you from the cold ground is just as important.

There are three types of sleeping pad:

(1) **Air pads.** These need to be inflated. Usually you blow them up with your breath, although you can also use a bag-style hand pump (usually sold separately). Some models feature a built-in hand pump. Air pads are comfortable, lightweight, and compact when packed. Most are designed for backpacking or camping in warm conditions (about 3 R-value), but some come with extra insulation for winter camping. You can customize the firmness of an air pad by releasing some air

from the valve while you're lying on it. They can be punctured or ripped (this is most common when sharing a tent with dogs), but field repairs are not difficult if you remember to bring along a repair kit. Also, moisture from your breath can get trapped inside an air pad, leading to freezing in winter or mold in summer. (Using a hand pump will help prevent moisture build-up.)

(2) **Self-inflating pads** are a combination of open-cell foam insulation and air. Open the pad's valve and air fills the chambers automatically. Some are specifically designed for backpacking and can be folded lengthwise and then rolled up to fit inside your pack. Others are designed for car camping and are rolled up without folding. They're comfortable and compact, they offer excellent insulation, and you can adjust their firmness by adding or releasing air. However they're heavier and more expensive than simple foam pads and not as compact as air pads. They can also be punctured or ripped.

(3) **Closed-cell foam pads.** These pads are made of dense foam filled with tiny closed air cells. They're usually rolled up or folded in a Z formation. They're lightweight, inexpensive, durable, and offer good insulation. You don't need to worry about punctures or leaks. However, they are less comfortable than air pads or self-inflating pads.

Air pads and self-inflating pads are both good choices for car camping. Closed-cell pads are mostly for backpackers.

When shopping for a sleeping pad, you should know about the following:

(1) **Insulation.** Even in summer, you lose body heat to the ground while you sleep. To counteract this, most air and self-inflating pads have a layer of synthetic insulation inside. A few pads have down insulation and are geared toward winter camping. A sleeping pad's R-value measures its capacity to resist (hence the "R") heat flow. The higher a pad's R-value, the better it will insulate you from the cold ground. R-values range from 1.0 (minimally insulated) to 9.5 (very well insulated). Thicker pads generally have higher R-values and the average summer camping pad has an R-value of around 3. Campers who sleep cold, often women, may want to choose a pad with a higher R-value—at least 4. Some women-specific pads put more insulation in the core and feet area where women lose heat fastest.

(2) **Size.** At a minimum, your shoulders and hips need to fit on the pad. Regular (typically 72 inches long) and long (typically 78 inches long) pads will insulate your legs and feet—a big plus on chilly fall and winter trips. Most pads are 20 inches wide, but if you're a large person or tend to roll around a lot, you may want a pad that is 25 or 30 inches wide. Some sleeping bags have a sleeve underneath to hold the pad. This keeps you and your sleeping bag from sliding off the pad in the night. If you have one of these sleeping bags, make sure the pad that you buy will fit into the sleeve.

(3) **Construction.** Some pads have larger side baffles, often called "rails," to cradle you and help keep you from rolling off as you turn during sleep. Some pads have a pillow baffle for your head. If you're a restless sleeper, look for a pad with a textured or brushed-fabric surface. This helps keep you and your sleeping bag from sliding off at night. You'll need a patch kit for an air and self-inflating pad. Find out whether one comes with the pad or is sold separately. Be sure you understand how to patch a puncture before you leave home, in case you have to repair one in the dark.

(4) **Inflation.** If you don't relish the idea of blowing up your sleeping pad after a long day of hiking, look for a pad with an integrated hand pump or purchase a bag-style hand pump. Some pads have both a high-volume inflation valve and a deflation valve, which can speed air flow in or out. Some pads have extra-large openings that allow fast inflation with fewer breaths. Pads with two or more independent air chambers can give you peace of mind. If one chamber fails, the others will still give you some cushioning.

For car camping, a *large inflatable air mattress* is an alternative to a sleeping pad. Big-box stores carry twin-sized air mattresses and such a mattress will fit nicely in a two-person tent. Air mattresses are heavy and bulky and they lack insulation, so they're best for summer camping. To inflate them, you will need a battery-powered air pump (usually sold separately). A note here: Be sure to buy a battery-pow-

ered pump, not one that you plug into an electrical outlet. There are no electrical outlets in the wilderness. Also
note that most battery-powered air pumps require big D
cell batteries. Be sure you take along plenty of fresh ones.
When you bring your new air mattress and air pump home,
fill the mattress with air and try it out. Here's how you inflate
it:

> (1) Open the valve cover. Most air mattresses
> have a one-way air valve (which allows air to
> enter the mattress, but not leave it). The valve
> is located somewhere on the side or end of the
> mattress. Find this valve and remove the protec-
> tive cap.

> (2) Insert the pump's nozzle into the valve open-
> ing. Most pumps come with several nozzles of
> different sizes. Select the size that fits the tightest
> in the valve. Switch on the pump and wait a few
> minutes for it to inflate the mattress.

> (3) Once the mattress is fully inflated, remove
> the pump and replace the valve cover. That's all
> there is to it!

What happens if you switch on your mattress pump and
nothing happens? The batteries are dead. Most people don't
know that it's possible to inflate an air mattress with nothing
more than a standard-size plastic garbage bag. To do this,
first open the bag and wave it up and down to catch plenty of
air. Gather up the open end of the bag to trap the air inside
and then wrap this open end tightly around the air valve of
your mattress. Squeeze the bag to force the air out and into
the mattress (it's often easiest to do this by slowly laying on
the bag). Repeat as needed. It might take a while to inflate

your mattress this way and you might not be able to get it fully inflated, but it beats sleeping on the hard ground.

:: ::

There's nothing better than spending the day hiking and the evening by a campfire while the cool air settles around you and then crawling into your luxuriously comfortable tent with an air mattress bed. That's how it's supposed to go anyway.

There was one time when I had hiked in a cold drizzle for most of the day. That night, a heavy rain pelted down. No campfire, just a tired woman who was damp and cold in the middle of nowhere with no heat and no cell phone service. I crawled into my tent, took off wet clothes, put on dry sweatpants and a dry sweatshirt, and snuggled into my bed. With a book and a lantern, I covered up and felt the warmth of my body heat surround me inside my sleeping bag and under my extra blankets. As the rain turned to sleet and then to quiet soft fat snowflakes, I slid deeper down into my warm bed and read my book until I fell asleep. I was warm and dry and slept all night long.

In the morning, I woke slowly to my breath steaming and several inches of snow covering the sides and roof of the tent. There was also an unpleasant dampness around my legs. I peeked out and saw the happy face of my dog, sitting by the tent door, wagging her tail, eager to go outside. When she woke up, she had pressed up against the wall of the tent and this had caused water to wick through the fabric and get inside. Waking

inside a wet tent wasn't the best way to start the day.
And trust me, it was even worse the next night.

■ ■
■ ■

Choosing Clothing

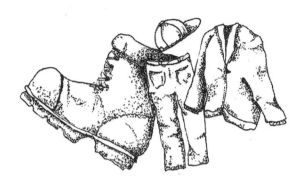

You know how to find a good campsite and you've got your tent, sleeping bag, and sleeping pad. Now let's talk about what you're going to wear. Your goal: Be prepared for anything—heat, cold, rain, snow, wind, mud, falling in the river ...anything. Your strategy: Layering—a tried-and-true method for staying comfortable by putting on or peeling off layers of clothing as your activity level or the weather changes.

There are three different layers of clothing, each with a specific purpose: (1) *a base (or underwear) layer* that wicks sweat off your skin, (2) *a middle (or insulating) layer* that retains body heat to protect you from the cold, (3) *an outer (or shell) layer* that shields you from wind and rain.

You won't be wearing all three layers all the time, of course, but it's a good idea to take them all with you on a camping trip. You can take off layers if you get too hot, but you can't put on layers that you didn't bring along.

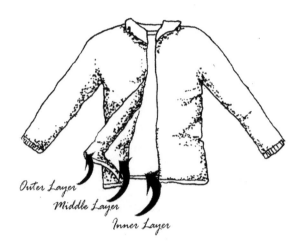

Outer Layer
Middle Layer
Inner Layer

The base (or underwear) layer. This is the next-to-skin layer and its job is to wick perspiration away from your skin. When you're camping in the cold, you need wicking long underwear to keep your skin dry. It comes in a wide range of fabrics, including synthetics like polyester and nylon and natural fibers like merino wool and silk.

Synthetic fabrics excel at wicking and dissipating sweat, so they give you the driest feel of any type of fabric. They are also the most durable. Some of them have a finish that inhibits the buildup of odor-causing bacteria, which helps to keep you smelling good. The most common synthetic fabric for long underwear is polyester. You might also see nylon, polypropylene, rayon, or a blend of these. Fabrics that include spandex offer comfortable stretch and can fit snugly without feeling constrictive.

Natural fabrics include merino wool and silk. Merino wool has almost completely replaced traditional wool in long underwear. It is sometimes blended with other fabrics, like spandex, to enhance fit and flexibility. Merino wool wicks well, but retains some moisture, so it won't keep you quite as dry as a synthetic fabric. It also takes longer to dry when it gets wet. Its best feature is that it is naturally resistant to odor-causing bacteria. Wool fanatics report endless days of sweaty wear without a discouraging whiff. Silk is also a base layer option if you don't plan to exert yourself. It's incredibly soft, but it's not especially durable and not naturally odor resistant, so it needs to be laundered every time you wear it.

To be able to wick sweat efficiently, your next-to-skin layer needs to actually be next to your skin. So a comfortably snug fit everywhere is your goal. Don't rely solely on marketing terms like "athletic fit." Try it on to be sure.

Long underwear might not be appealing when temperatures soar, but having dry skin makes you more comfortable even when it's hot. A summer shirt works as a base layer. Look for ones that offer wicking. They won't really be marketed as a base layer, but as your next-to-skin layer they can increase your comfort in hot conditions. Underwear like briefs, boxers and bras should also wick (the same is true when you wear it under your long underwear in winter). Cotton fabric is considered a no-no in cool weather because it sponges up water, but it can be okay if you're camping on a super-dry, scorching summer day.

The middle (or insulating) layer helps you retain the heat that's radiated by your body. The more efficiently this layer traps that heat, the warmer you'll be. You have a broad range of options, both synthetic and natural. In general, thicker (or puffier) equals warmer, though the efficiency of the insulating material is also important.

Polyester fleece is available in lightweight, midweight, and heavyweight fabrics (sometimes marketed as 100, 200 and 300 weight). It stays warm even if gets damp, and it dries fast. Fleece also breathes well, so you're less likely to overheat in it. The flipside of breathability, though, is that wind blows right through, which can steal warmth. That's why you need to have a shell layer with you if you're going with a fleece middle layer.

Down-insulated jackets are highly compressible for easy packing. Down offers more warmth for its weight than any other insulating material. The efficiency of down is measured in fill power—from 450 to 900. The drawback is that down loses insulating efficiency when damp. The outside layer of a down jacket is always made of water- and wind-resistant material, so these jackets can serve as both a middle and outer layer if the weather isn't too bad.

Synthetic-insulated jackets have long tried to mimic down's insulating efficiency and are getting better all the time. And while synthetics don't compress as well as down, they're a popular option for rainy conditions because they retain insulating ability when they get damp. The outer layer of a synthetic-insulated jacket is also made of water- and wind-resistant material, so like down jackets, they can serve as both a middle and outer layer in mild weather.

Cotton may not be the fabric of choice for the layer against your skin, but nothing beats a nice warm cotton sweat suit when the sun goes down and the campfire is crackling. It isn't for hot weather or strenuous activity and it takes a long time for cotton to dry, especially in humid areas. Wool makes a great middle layer if you're camping in really cold weather. It keeps the heat in, has a natural wicking ability, and is resistant to odor-causing bacteria. Pack a wool shirt or sweater and a wool knit cap. A wool cap is compact and it goes on your head where you lose most of your body heat.

The outer (or shell) layer protects you from wind, rain and snow. Shells range from pricey mountaineering jackets to simple windbreakers. Most of them allow at least some perspiration to escape and virtually all are treated with a durable water repellent (DWR) finish to make water bead up and roll off the fabric. They can be categorized as follows:

Waterproof, breathable shells are your most functional (and most expensive) choice. This type of shell is your best option for really stormy conditions. Generally, pricier equals drier.

Water-resistant, breathable shells are more suited to drizzly, breezy conditions and high activity levels. More affordable than waterproof/breathable shells, they're typically made of tightly woven nylon or polyester fabric that blocks light wind and light rain.

Waterproof, non-breathable shells are bare-bones shells that are okay for rainy days with light to no activity (e.g., fishing). They are typically made of coated nylon, which is waterproof and windproof. If you exert yourself while wearing one of these shells, you'll probably end up saturating your underneath layers with perspiration.

Soft shells emphasize breathability. Most feature stretch fabric or fabric panels for added comfort during aerobic activities. Many combine light rain and wind protection with light insulation, so they are in effect middle and outer layers in a single jacket.

Don't forget socks. Socks are the one item you should not skimp on. Here are some things to consider:

Two layers. Consider wearing two layers of socks, especially when it's cold outside and you're going to be doing a lot of hiking. The outer layer will be your hiking socks. The inner layer will be made of thin moisture-wicking fabric that helps keep your feet dry and less susceptible to blisters.

Height. Hiking socks come in different heights. To choose the right height, take a look at your boots. No-show socks should only be worn with low-cut footwear, like trail-running shoes or light hiking shoes.Ankle-length socks are good for low- to mid-cut shoes and boots. Crew-length socks typically land a few inches above your ankle bones to protect against abrasion with boots with high cuffs. You can also wear them with low-cut boots or shoes, but know that they can make your feet too warm on a hot day. Knee-high socks protect against abrasion that big, burly boots can cause around your shins and calves. You won't need knee-high socks unless you plan to go mountaineering.

Cushioning. The amount of cushioning a hiking sock gives you depends on how thick it is and determines how warm it will be. The right amount of cushioning for you depends mostly on the types of hiking you plan to do and the weather you expect to encounter. A bit of cushion can protect your feet during high-impact activities like trail running, but keep in mind that thick socks can cause your feet to sweat. You may have to experiment to find the right balance of cushion-to-warmth that works for you. Having a variety of socks to choose from in your sock drawer is helpful.

Fabric. Never cotton: It retains moisture. Wool is the most popular hiking sock material and the one that footwear specialists recommend above all others. It regulates temperature well to keep your feet from getting sweaty and it provides cushioning. Another plus is that wool is naturally antimicrobial so it tends to retain smells less than synthetic fabrics. These days most socks are made of merino wool, which is essentially itch-free compared to older types of rag wool socks. Most wool socks are actually blends of wool and synthetic materials for better durability and faster drying. Polyester is a synthetic material that insulates, wicks moisture and dries quickly. It is sometimes blended with wool and/or nylon to create a good combination of warmth, comfort, durability and fast drying. Many hiking socks include a small percentage of spandex. This elastic material helps socks hold their shape and keep bunching and wrinkling to a minimum.

Fit. If your socks are too big, they can have wrinkles that will rub and may cause a blister. Too small and they can create pressure points and sock slippage. When you try socks on, look for a snug, but not overly tight fit. A sock fits properly when the heel cup lines up with the heel of your foot.

And a few more things. How about a swimsuit? A bandana? A pair of gloves? A clothes line to hang up wet clothes? An oven mitt so you won't burn your hands on hot campfire pots?

Bring a change of clothing for each day of camping. You'll have them even if you don't wear them. Also bring at least one pair of dry, clean socks for each day. Changing to dry socks when you get back to camp is one of the supreme pleasures of camping. Spare socks also come in handy if your feet get soaked while crossing a stream. Remember that every single piece of clothing you take camping will require washing when you get home unless you want to smell like a campfire. Even clothes you don't wear will smell like a campfire.

∷

One year I was camping in the spring. On the first day, I hiked for a couple of miles and ended up that night sleeping in the same pants I had worn hiking. It was warmer the next day, so I popped into my tent to change into a pair of shorts. To my surprise and dismay, there was a tick embedded in my calf. If I had changed into clean clothes as soon as I got back to camp on the previous day, I would have found the tick and removed it sooner.

I camped on a riverbank one spring and it was chilly, maybe in the 40s during the day and below freezing at night. The water temperature was about 40 degrees. I set up camp and went fishing on the edge of a deep pool in the river. It was early in the spring and the water was flowing fast with snowmelt. I knew the river held big trout and hoped to catch one. I was wearing waders over a layer of thick warm clothing. I edged out into the water and stood at the edge of a big drop off in the river. The water was up to my knees, but within a few inches of my toes the river bottom dropped down into a pool about 12 feet deep.

Suddenly the edge I was standing on collapsed and I was in the river. The current was strong and pulled me along. My waders filled with water and started pulling me under. I never got the chance to panic though, because I soon slammed into a downed tree lying across the river and had the air knocked out of me. Eventually

I pulled myself up the tree trunk to the shore, pulled off my water-filled waders, and stumbled back up the river to a spot shallow enough to cross back to my campsite. I started shivering immediately and my hands were numb. By the time I got back to my campsite, I was frozen. There was no one else around. I stripped off all of my wet clothes right there in front of my tent and crawled in completely naked because I didn't want to drag all that heavy, sopping clothing into the tent with me. I dug warm dry clothes out of my bag and buried myself in the sleeping bag until I stopped shivering. Of course it was my fault for wading too far out and not wearing a wading belt to the keep the water from filling up my waders. Luckily I'd brought two full sets of warm heavy clothing and spent the rest of the night sitting by the campfire wondering if I ever wanted to tell anyone I'd been careless and almost drowned because of it. I haven't waded that river since.

∶∶

Choosing Shoes

You won't be sitting around camp in the daytime. You'll be out hiking, trail-running, fishing, canoeing, kayaking, bird-watching, taking photographs—whatever is your passion. No matter how you spend your day, you'll be spending much of it on your feet in rough terrain, so a pair of good hiking boots is important, probably the most important item in your camping kit and the one you'll spend the most money on.

The type of boot you choose will depend on the type of activity you have in mind. There are four main types of hiking boot:

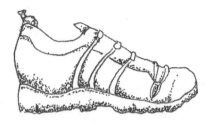

(1) *Trail runners*, designed for running on hiking trails. They are basically road-running shoes with beefed-up stiffness, cushioning, and soles with thick lugs to provide traction in soft soil and mud.

(2) *Hiking shoes*, low-cut shoes with flexible mid-soles designed for easy hiking on hiking trails.

(3) *Day hiking boots*, mid- to high-cut boots intended for all-day hiking.

(4) *High-cut boots* designed for multiday trips
deep into the backcountry, on or off the trail.

Hiking shoes or day hiking boots are the best choice for most
car-campers, although trail runners are also suitable, especially if the weather is hot or if you actually participate in trail
running as a sport. High-cut boots are for serious mountaineering.

Buying boots that fit. You shouldn't buy hiking shoes or
boots online unless you're buying the exact brand and size
you've worn before. Otherwise, you should go to an outdoor
store and try them on before buying. It's best to shop for
boots late in the day (your feet swell during the day and are at
their largest in the afternoon) and try them on while wearing
the same socks you plan to wear when you go hiking. Take a
stroll through the store. Walk up and down stairs. Find an in-
clined surface and walk on that. Hiking boots should fit snug
everywhere, be tight nowhere, and offer room to wiggle your
toes. You don't want to feel odd bumps or seams, or pinching
in the forefoot, or toes hitting the end of the boot. If the boots
are laced firmly and you can still feel space above the top of
your foot, then the volume of the boot is wrong.

Breaking in your boots. When you get home, wear your

boots around the house. Wear the socks you'll be wearing on the trail and tie your boots snugly, but not too tight. Make sure the tongues and gussets are straight. Your new boots will be a little stiff at first, which is fine. Walk around the block and around town. Make sure your boots still feel good and gradually increase the distance. Finally hit the trail. Off pavement is where serious breaking in happens. Gradually increase the mileage.

Adjusting the fit. When you're out on the trail, your boots may start to slip or hurt your feet. Sometimes you can solve the problem simply by changing the way you lace them up.

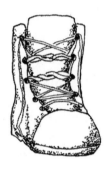

(1) If your heel is slipping excessively, your boot is probably too loose at the top of your foot. You can cinch it down and hold it in place with two surgeon's knots. These knots hold fast and won't work themselves loose. Unlace your boot down to where the top of your foot begins to flex forward and tie a surgeon's knot (that is, wrap the laces around each other twice), then pull the laces tight, run them up to the next hook, and tie another surgeon's knot. Finish lacing the rest of your boot in your usual way.

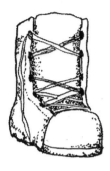

(2) If you feel too much pressure on the top of your foot, window lacing (also called "box lacing") can help alleviate the problem. Unlace your boot down to the hooks just below the pressure point, then re-lace them by going straight up to the next hook and then crossing the laces over. Finish lacing the rest of your boot in your usual way.

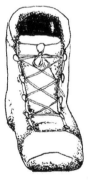

(3) If your toes hurt, you can open up the toe box of your boot using this trick. Completely unlace your boot. Then lace it back up—but skip the first set of hooks. (If your toes always hurt when you hike, you might need a different pair of boots.)

Blisters. Pay close attention to how your feet feel when you're hiking. The minute you sense an uncomfortable spot, stop and take your boots and socks off. If the area is even slightly red, then dry it off and apply one of the following products: (1) *Dr. Scholl's Moleskin*, the classic cut-to-size blister-coverage product; similar products do the same thing but go by different names, (2) *Anti-chafing balm*, such as Body Glide, (3) *Tape*, such as "tear-to-size" paper surgeon's tape or other cloth or synthetic medical tapes or even duct tape, in a pinch.

If that hot spot develops into a full-blown blister, you have a few options: (1) *Dr. Scholl's Molefoam padding* with a doughnut hole. Cut a large enough hole in the Molefoam padding for the blister and apply it. The surrounding foam should keep your sock from rubbing and further irritating the area. For more protection, you can add a layer of Dr. Scholl's Moleskin or tape on top. (2) *Pads and Gels.* Both are designed to add a protective layer to prevent a blister from getting worse. Pads also provide cushioning; gels soothe the area by cooling it off. (3) *Drain the blister.* Do this only as a last resort. You're creating a chance for infection and you're removing the protection and healing that the serum inside the blister provides. However if you have a large blister that's too painful to leave undrained, then sterilize a needle with alcohol or heat, insert it near the base of the blister, and let the fluid drain out. Then dress the blister like you would a wound, using antibiotic ointment and gauze or a Band-Aid. Cut and place Dr. Scholl's Molefoam padding with a doughnut hole around the area to prevent further irritation. For added protection, add a layer of tape over the top.

Camp shoes. At the end of a long day on the trail, what could be better than kicking off your boots? Your campsite is probably full of rocks and roots and poison ivy, so you can't walk around barefoot. You might want to bring along a second pair of shoes. Flip flops, sandals, tennis shoes and water shoes are options. A shoe with a closed toe would be better than flip flops for protecting your feet. Some campers, especially those who use trail runners, opt not to bring camp shoes. Trail runners are so light and comfortable that you can wear them all day. Problem is: If your trail runners get wet out on the trail, you won't have any dry shoes to change into.

∎ ∎
∎ ∎

I once started to hike a trail that started across the river from my campsite. I loaded up my backpack with snacks and water, leashed my dog, and hung a pair of hiking boots over my shoulder. We waded to the middle of the river with no problem, but as we approached the far bank, I noticed that the current had slowed and the color of the river bottom had changed from light tan to black. My dog was about 10 feet ahead of me. All of the sudden he let out a yelp and went under. He promptly bobbed back up and started swimming, but not in his usual graceful way. Instead, he thrashed around and rolled his eyes and appeared to be trying to walk without being able to get any footing. Quicksand! Well, not exactly quicksand—it was black, smelly ooze that collects in low spots of the river. If you step in it, you just sink. I immediately let go of the leash and threw myself backward away from the black hole and ended up sitting in the water. Eventually both of us made it to the far bank. I tossed my backpack and boots on the ground, rinsed off my waders in the river, and put on my socks and hiking boots. Only trouble was, every-

thing was soaking wet. I tried to continue hiking up the trail, but before long my wet boots and socks got so uncomfortable that I had to turn around and slog back across the river to my campsite. You can't hike in wet shoes and socks.

■ ■
■ ■

Building a Campfire

You're going to want a campfire. But wait a minute! Make sure you are permitted to build a fire where you plan to camp. In dry seasons, the government may ban all campfires to avoid forest fires. You can check by visiting the Department of Natural Resources website of your state or call the campground directly if they have a phone number. Always build your campfire in the fire ring. There's one at every campsite.

To start a campfire, you'll need three types of fuel—*tinder*, *kindling*, and *firewood*.

(1) *Tinder* is highly flammable material, such as small twigs, dry leaves, needles, or forest duff. You may be able to gather tinder at the campsite, but don't count on it. Often you will find that the entire campsite has been picked clean of flammable material by previous campers, so it's a good

47

idea to bring tinder from home. Dryer lint or toilet paper are good choices.

(2) *Kindling* consists of small sticks about the size of a pencil. Don't count on finding kindling at the campsite either. You may have to split your own from bigger pieces of firewood. Bring an axe.

(3) *Firewood* is larger pieces of wood that will keep your fire going long into the night. Try not to burn pieces thicker than your wrist. Instead split them with your axe. Thick chunks of wood rarely burn completely and you may be left with blackened, unsightly scraps in the morning. Note that you may not be allowed to bring firewood from home. In many states, transporting firewood over long distances is illegal because it may carry invasive insects that destroy trees. So you may have to buy bundles of firewood from vendors near your campsite. Oak and maple are best. Avoid birch and poplar. Carefully inspect the wood you plan to buy to make sure it has been properly seasoned. Freshly-cut firewood has lots of moisture in it and will not burn. It will smoke a lot, but it will not produce flame and you'll end up with a smoking, hissing fire. The firewood you want to buy was cut at least one year ago and allowed to dry out. Here are a couple of things to help you identify seasoned wood: It has been split. (Whole logs never really dry out.) It is "checked," that is, it has tiny cracks at the cut ends. (Freshly-cut firewood is smooth at the ends.) It is light in weight. (Wet firewood is dense and heavy.) If it has a weathered grey color

and has spider webs on it, so much the better.

Laying a Campfire. You can assemble tinder, kindling and firewood in various ways. Here are a few of them:

(1) *Teepee:* Start with a small cone of kindling around a few handfuls of tinder loosely piled in the center of the fire ring. Once the fire is going strong, add larger logs a few at a time.

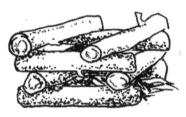

(2) *Log cabin:* Place two larger pieces of firewood parallel to each other with some room in between them to form a base. Then place two slightly smaller pieces on top of and perpendicular to the first two to form a square. Place plenty of tinder inside the square. Continue adding more layers of firewood around the perimeter, getting a little bit smaller with each layer. Finish with a layer of kindling and tinder across the top.

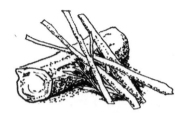

(3) *Lean-to:* The lean-to is built with a log (or dry stone) as a prop to hold up kindling that is leaned against it. Place tinder underneath the kindling. This is my preferred method for several reasons: the fuel log can act as a wind break or wind scoop, it is a very stable structure and the fuel log is immediately heated for quicker ignition.

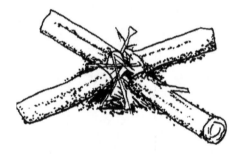

(4) *Star:* This is another classic campfire that works quite well. Firewood is placed like spokes in a wheel, leaving an opening at the center for a mound of tinder and kindling. The logs provide the same benefit as a lean-to with the added advantage that the logs can vary in length and be pushed into the center as they are consumed by the fire. This comes in handy when you are unable to cut firewood into equal lengths.

(5) *Pyramid:* Start with three or four of your largest logs side-by-side on the bottom layer. Add a second layer of slightly smaller logs on top of and perpendicular to the bottom layer. Continue alternating a few more layers in this manner, getting smaller as you go. Place your kindling and tinder on top.

Lighting a Campfire. Laying the fire was the hard part. Now comes your reward—you get to light it. Strike a match or lighter and hold it under the tinder. Blow lightly on the tinder to provide oxygen, which will help increase the intensity of the flame and ignite the kindling and finally the wood. As the fire burns, move embers to the center to burn them completely. If you have chosen the right firewood and laid it properly, you will soon have a crackling fire that lasts for hours with nothing left but white ash at bedtime.

You go to light the fire and your lighter doesn't work or your matches are wet! Not to worry; you can still light the fire. Here's how:

(1) First make a tinder nest. It will be used to create the flame from the ember you're about to create.

(2) Now you have to create an ember. The easi-

est way to do this is with a *flint and steel set*. You really should buy one of these sets and take it with you when you go camping. When shopping for a flint and steel set, look for one that includes a *char cloth*, that is, a cloth that has been turned into charcoal. The char cloth catches the spark created by striking steel against flint and keeps it smoldering without bursting into flame. If you don't have a char cloth, a piece of dry fungus or birch might also work. To create the ember, take hold of the flint and char cloth between your thumb and forefinger with the edge hanging out about 2 or 3 inches. Strike the steel against the flint several times. Sparks from the steel will fly off and land on the char cloth, causing it to glow. Place the char cloth into the tinder nest and gently blow on it to start a flame.

(3) If it's sunny out, you can create an ember by using some sort of lens or reflector to focus sunlight onto the tinder nest. A magnifying glass, eyeglasses, or binocular lens will work. You can intensify the beam by putting some water on the lens. The reflector out of your flashlight or even the polished bottom of a soda can will also work. Angle the lens (or reflector) towards the sun and focus the beam into as small an area as possible. Put your tinder nest under this spot and you'll soon have yourself a fire.

(4) You can also make an ember with batteries and steel wool. Spread out the steel wool. (You want it to be about 6 inches long and ½-inch wide.) Hold the steel wool in one hand and the

battery in the other. Any battery will do, but a 9-volt battery works best. Rub the side of the battery with the contacts against the wool. The wool will begin to glow and burn. Gently blow on it. Transfer the burning steel wool to your tinder nest. The steel wool's flame will extinguish quickly, so don't waste any time.

(5) As a last resort, you can create an ember by rubbing two pieces of wood together. This method is not for the faint of heart—it takes a lot of rubbing. First you'll need to make a wooden fireboard and spindle. The wood must be bone dry. Find a flat board for the fireboard and cut a lengthwise groove in it. Then find a stick a foot or two feet long and about an inch in diameter for the spindle. Place the tinder nest at the end of the groove. Now rub the spindle back and forth in the groove until friction produces an ember. Blow lightly on the ember until the tinder bursts into flame.

When it's time to pack up and go home, extinguish your campfire by pouring water on it, stirring the ashes, then applying more water. Repeat as often as needed. Ashes should be cool to the touch before you leave the campsite. Be utterly certain a fire is out before you depart. Burn trash in the fire pit only if it can be fully consumed by fire and turned to ash before you leave. If you do burn something that's not fully consumed, collect the remains when the fire is out and put it in a trash receptacle. Do not attempt to burn plastic, metal cans, or foil.

■ ■
■ ■

There's a campground near Lake Michigan where I have camped several times. The first time I went up there, I bought some unseasoned wood from a roadside stand and ended up with a hissing fire that night. The next day I drove around looking for dry firewood and stopped at a different roadside stand. The proprietor was standing in his yard and hollered a hello. I hollered a hello back and told him I wanted to buy a bundle of firewood, but he said the wood in his firewood stand was only a few months old and not yet seasoned. He told me to pull my vehicle around the back of this barn and there I found a covered woodshed filled with well-seasoned ash and oak. I loaded up some of the oak and offered to pay him twice his roadside price, but he brushed aside my outstretched cash. "Keep it," he said, "Buy yourself some extra beer," and sent me on my way. It rained that night, but I hardly noticed as I sat beside my blazing campfire of free dry oak. You never know whom you'll meet when you're camping.

■ ■
■ ■

Preparing Meals

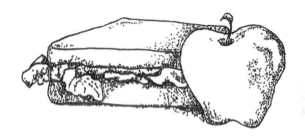

You're camping alone—you can eat whatever you want. Hot-dogs and chips. Filet mignon and asparagus.

I love cooking over the campfire on my grill, which is basically a grate on a pole. I pound the pole into the ground beside the fire and swing the grate over the fire after I get it going. My grill is all charred up and dirty, but I use it every time I go camping and I can turn out some good chow. After I cook, I leave the grate over the fire to burn off any stuck-on food.

When I don't feel like cooking over the campfire, I cook on a camp stove. You may remember the old Coleman camp stoves that your parents had that burned white gas, but nowadays there are better alternatives. I prefer camp stoves that burn propane gas that comes in a small canister. If you go to the outdoor section of Wal-Mart, you will find propane stoves—one-burner or two-burner. You will also find those little green canisters of propane. Make sure you get a propane stove. There are stoves that burn other types of fuel, but propane stoves are best, because fuel canisters for them are available at grocery stores and gas stations everywhere.

It's easy to hook up the propane canister to the stove. First make sure all of the burner valve(s) on the stove are turned all the way off. Then simply screw the end of the stove's fuel tube onto the nozzle on the gas canister. The canister won't release any propane gas until it is screwed on tight, so it's tough to mess up. Then hold a lighter or a match to the burner, (or to the first burner if there are more than one) and slowly open its valve. Remember to light your lighter or strike your match before opening the gas valve. That way you catch the first gas to escape from the burner and avoid a mini-explosion. After the burner is lit, adjust the flame and you're ready to cook.

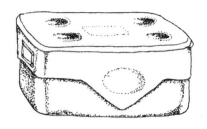

You'll need a cooler to transport and store any food that needs to be kept cold. Buy the best five-day cooler you can afford. They are called "five-day coolers" because they're supposed keep your food cold for five days, although mine never keeps food cold that long—more like two or three days.

Now comes the fun part. Make out a menu of the meals you want to eat. (If you need suggestions, I've listed some of my favorite recipes below.) Then make a list of groceries you'll need to prepare these meals and a list of required kitchen equipment—things like skillets, pots, tinfoil, zip-lock bags, cups, paper towels, a knife. Also things you'll need for cleanup—a sponge, a scratchy thing, a container of soap and/or bleach and water mix.

When you're ready to go camping, put all condiments (butter, mustard, salad dressing, etc.) in zip-lock bags to keep the water out. Pre-cook all meats—then you can just heat them up and brown them off at the campsite. If you want eggs, break them open and pour them into a sealed jar before leaving so they are easy to pour into the pan and won't get crushed in the cooler. Cut up veggies and bag them up before you leave. You could cut up veggies at a campsite, but it's a lot easier if you bring them already chopped up. Never rely on "re-sealable" packaging; it always lets water in. Seal everything you put in the cooler in a zip-lock bag and bring extra zip-lock bags for leftovers.

Bring paper plates. They make good food-prep surfaces and

you can burn them afterward in the campfire. If you plan to cook over the campfire, a cast iron skillet works best. If you plan to cook on the camp stove, use a non-stick skillet. Just before you're about to leave for the campground, dump ice in your cooler, take the cold food out of the refrigerator, and put it on top of the ice. Close the top and keep it closed until you're ready to cook. You will have to replenish ice in the cooler after a couple of days. Be sure to drain out the water before putting in new ice.

Don't forget to bring water from home. Most of the water you'll find in the wilderness isn't fit to drink. You'll need a minimum of a gallon of water per day to be comfortable. I drink about half a gallon, use a quarter of a gallon for coffee and then brush my teeth and wash/rinse dishes and my hands with the rest. You may find water at your campsite. If it is marked 'potable', that means you can drink it. If it isn't marked 'potable', don't drink it. You can buy water by the gallon at the grocery store or to save money, wash out gallon jugs and fill them with tap water in your sink at home. I always take two gallons of water from home and then if I need more, I refill the jugs in the closest town if I can find safe water or buy more bottled water.

Coffee! If you want coffee (and I always want coffee), you'll need to bring a coffee pot. I use a percolator on the campfire and on my propane stove. I pour the amount of water I want into the bottom of the percolator pot. Then I add one tablespoon of coarse-ground coffee per cup of water in the top chamber. I place the percolator on the fire and heat the water to just before boiling (actually boiling the water can lead to over-extraction and bitter coffee). When the pot begins "perking" (making the characteristic blub-blub noise), the coffee is ready to drink. If you prefer to make pour-over or French press or instant coffee or tea, you can use the percolator (without the upper chamber) to heat the water.

Here are some of my favorite recipes:

Campfire Nachos

Ingredients:
- Tortilla chips
- Nacho cheese or cheese dip (optional)
- Amendments, such as olives, jalapenos, etc.
- Shredded cheese
- Toppings, such as sour cream, hot sauce, etc.

Directions:
1. Spread out the chips in an iron skillet
2. Add nacho cheese.
3. Add ammendments

4. Sprinkle on shredded cheese.
5. Bake next to the campfire until the chips are warm and the cheese is melted.
6. Remove from the fire and add toppings.

Campfire Mac 'n' Cheese

Ingredients:
- ½ cup uncooked elbow macaroni
- 1 cup Alfredo sauce
- ½ cup grated sharp cheddar cheese
- ½ cup grated Parmesan cheese
- ¼ cup mozzarella cheese
- ¼-½ cup half and half or whole milk
- Salt and pepper, to taste

Directions:
At home:
1. Cook pasta according to package directions.
2. Stir Alfredo sauce and three cheeses into the cooked pasta. Add enough milk to make it a little runny, but not soupy. Stir in salt and pepper to taste. Spray small individual pie tins with non-stick cooking spray and fill them with mac and cheese. Spray one side of aluminum foil sheets with more nonstick cooking spray and cover each pie tin, sprayed side down. Refrigerate until ready to cook.

At Camp:
1. Prepare a fire and let it burn down to the coals. Place pie tins over the hot coals and cook until hot (about 10 minutes).

Campfire Chili Cheese Fries

Ingredients:
- 1 package frozen French fries
- 1 can chili
- 1 cup shredded cheddar cheese

Directions:
1. Spray the inside of a large sheet of foil with cooking spray.
2. Place the frozen fries in the middle of the sheet; fold tightly to enclose.
3. Cook the fries over a campfire until they are cooked (about 20 minutes).
4. Spread the chili and cheese over the fries.
5. Close the packet again and cook until the chili is hot and the cheese is melted.

Breakfast Burritos

Ingredients:
- ½ tablespoon olive oil
- ½ cup frozen hash browns
- 4 oz. cooked ham, diced
- 6 eggs
- ½ tablespoon taco seasoning
- ½ 4.5 oz. can of green chilies
- 1 cup shredded cheddar cheese
- 1 tablespoon chopped cilantro
- 4 12-inch flour tortillas

Directions:
At Home:
1. Heat the olive oil in a large skillet. Add the hash

browns and cook for 1 minute, stirring continuously. Add the ham. Continue to cook, stirring occasionally, until the hash browns and ham have browned, about 8-10 minutes.

2. Meanwhile, in a large bowl, whisk the eggs. Stir in the taco seasoning. After the hash browns and ham have browned, pour the eggs into the skillet. Cook, stirring frequently, until the eggs have set. Stir in the green chilies, cheese, and cilantro.

3. Warm the tortillas. Pour ¼ of the egg mixture down the center of each tortilla. Roll up the burritos and wrap each one tightly in foil. Store burritos in a zip-lock bag and refrigerate. This recipe makes 4 burritos.

At Camp:

1. When ready to cook, place wrapped burritos in hot coals next to fire. Let the burritos sit in the coals, turning once, until heated through (about 15 minutes).

Steamed Salmon and Mushrooms

Ingredients:
- 4 ounces salmon
- 5 ounces mushrooms
- 2 teaspoons soy sauce
- ½ tablespoon unsalted butter
- Cilantro (for garnish)

Directions:
At Home:

1. Place the salmon on a large rectangular piece of aluminum foil.
2. Pile the mushrooms on top of the salmon.

3. Drizzle with the soy sauce and butter.
4. Fold the foil over the top of the salmon and seal the edges.
5. Place in zip-lock bag and refrigerate until ready to cook.

At Camp:
1. Add ¼-inch of water to a frying pan and add the pouch of salmon and mushrooms. Cover and bring to a boil. Reduce the heat to maintain a gentle simmer and steam until the salmon is cooked through (about 10 minutes). When the salmon is done, remove it from the pan, unwrap and garnish with cilantro.

Basic Omelet

Ingredients:
- 3 large eggs
- Coarse salt and ground pepper
- 1 tablespoon chopped scallions and/or fresh herbs such as parsley, tarragon, chives, dill, or cilantro (optional)
- 1 tablespoon butter
- ¼ cup of filling (onion or shallots, mushrooms, peppers, spinach, diced turkey or ham, crumbled bacon, chopped asparagus, cheese, diced tomatoes, prepared salsa, chopped canned artichoke hearts, etc.)

Directions:
1. In a medium bowl, whisk eggs until they are foamy. Add salt and pepper. Whisk in scallions and/or herbs, if desired.
2. Heat butter in an 8-inch nonstick skillet over

medium-high heat, tilting to coat pan; after foaming subsides, whisk eggs again, and add to skillet.

3. Cook, stirring quickly with a heatproof rubber spatula, until eggs begin to thicken (about 30 seconds). With spatula, pull edges of omelet in toward center, tilting pan so uncooked eggs flow to edges of pan and underneath omelet. Cook until just set but still loose (about 30 seconds more).

4. Sprinkle on the filling. Using a spatula, loosen omelet from skillet on all sides; shake pan to ensure it is completely released. Tilt pan toward serving plate; with spatula, working from side of skillet that's tilted up, fold 1/3 of omelet over the center.

5. Simultaneously slide and roll omelet onto plate so that it folds over on itself again and lands seam side down.

Omelet in a Bag

Ingredients:
- 2 eggs
- ½ cup of omelet filling of your choice (sausage, bacon, onions, mushrooms, peppers, etc.)
- ¼ cup of cheese

Directions:
1. Crack eggs into a quart-sized freezer bag.
2. Add fillings and cheese.
3. Seal bag and shake to scramble and mix the ingredients.
4. Cook in gently boiling water for 14-15 minutes.

■ ■
■ ■

I have always been leery of hand-pump wells in busy campgrounds because so many people are using them. People wash dishes and dirty boots and I've seen a family rinsing down their kayaks under the drinking water pump. Generally I bring a gallon or two of water for drinking and use water from the hand-pump water for washing and coffee. (It's safe for coffee because it's boiled). I tend to think that the more remote a campground is, the better the water must be, but recently I was camping in a campground out in the middle of nowhere and went to get water from the hand-pump well and right in the drain grille of the pump was a dead mouse. I drove thirty minutes to buy water. No way was I drinking water from that well. On the other hand, I've also had some of the best water I've ever tasted from hand-pump campground wells. High up on a bluff in the Upper Peninsula of Michigan, there is a hand-pump well in a little used corner of a state park. It has the sweetest water I've ever tasted and makes some of the best coffee I've ever had. I've filled up many gallon jugs there and have even filled up jugs to take home with me.

Occasionally I've been able to make a meal from things in the forest. On one trip, I caught a nice trout and gathered morel mushrooms and wild leeks. I cleaned the fish, tucked the mushrooms and leeks inside, and grilled it on the campfire grate. The next evening I was so tired out from hiking that I cooked a hotdog over the fire on a stick, tucked it in a bun, and slathered it with mustard. When you're camping, everything tastes delicious.

∷

Staying Warm and Dry

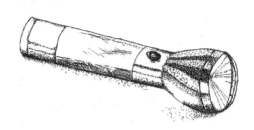

Pitching your tent. As soon as you get to your campsite, find a place to pitch your tent. Look for a place that is flat. It's uncomfortable to sleep on a slope. If possible, try to find high ground. Avoid dry creek beds, little divots, and hollows. If it rains hard, you don't want to wake up in a puddle. Ideally, you should place your tent so that it will remain in shade throughout the following morning, especially if it's hot. And it's also a good idea to find as much of a wind break as possible, in case the weather should pick up while you're out hiking. Placing your tent to the west of a hillside or a tree line is the best way of giving yourself a comfortable night inside and a cool morning to follow. Situate your tent away from the fire pit, ideally upwind from it. It's also smart to place your tent upwind from the outhouse. Once you've chosen the best spot, spend a few minutes clearing out any rocks and branches before setting up your tent.

Keeping your tent dry inside. The gentle pitter patter of rain on your rain fly is soothing, but water dripping inside your tent, that's really unpleasant. The culprit is condensation. Here's how to minimize it:

67

(1) *Pitch your tent under a tree.* Air under trees tends to be warmer than it is out in the open, so your rain fly will be warmer, too. In addition, condensation will occur mostly on the tree foliage instead of on your tent.

(2) *Minimize moisture inside your tent.* This moisture comes from three places: (1) the moisture in the air itself, that is, the humidity level, (2) moisture added by your breathing during the night, and (3) moisture added by wet stuff inside your tent. You can't control the humidity of the air and not breathing at night isn't really an option, but you can control how much wet stuff you allow inside your tent. Dry your wet clothes outside and try to dry the dog off as much as possible before letting it sleep in your tent.

(3) V*entilate.* Air inside the tent is almost always more humid than the surrounding air, so you want to replace the interior air with the drier outside air. Here's what you can do: (1) if there's a gentle breeze, pitch the tent so the door is facing into it, (2) stake the tent out tautly and tension the fly in order to maximize the airspace between it and the walls of the tent, (3) open all rain fly doors and rollup sections and close them only if rain starts to fall, and (4) open up all tent windows.

Keeping clean. Water is a precious commodity at the campsite, but you can wash up without water by using face wipes. You won't be wearing makeup, so it's fairly quick and easy. Other than makeup and a shower, you can pretty much perform all of your normal daily routines. On the first day at camp, wear your hair however you want. On the second day, a ponytail is just fine. After the second day, wear a baseball cap and keep wearing it on subsequent days until you can get a shower. You should bring at least two cups—one for water and one for coffee, and use the water cup to rinse out your mouth after you've brushed your teeth. Where's the sink for spitting that water into, you ask? Spit that froth right into the fire pit. No need to be demure. You're camping.

Restroom facilities at campgrounds are best described as "rustic" unless you stay in one of those fancy camps with a shower and you don't want to do that. Bring your own toilet paper and prepare to pay the price for some solitude. Will the outdoor toilet be stinky and gross? To be honest, it depends on the temperature, but the answer usually is, "Yes." You'll just have to put up with it. If worse comes to worse and you need to make a run into town, stop at McDonald's—they always have the cleanest restrooms.

Getting ready for bed. Store all of your food in your car. Toothpaste, deodorant, and lotions smell like food to bears and raccoons, so store them in your car along with your food. Take care not to be sloppy with food or trash. If camping where bears are active, do not sleep in clothes that may have absorbed food odors. Change out of any dirty or sweaty clothes. A good sleepwear choice is clean long underwear, top and bottoms, plus clean socks. Avoid overdressing before you hop in the bag, even if it's really cold outside. Wearing bulky clothing inside a sleeping bag actually reduces the bag's ability to trap body heat. Instead drape bulky items such as jackets over the top of your bag for an extra layer of insulation. Or bring an old comforter from home to serve as an extra layer.

Pee twice before going to bed. Some campers, women in particular, recommend going 20–30 minutes before bed and then again immediately before getting into your sleeping bag. This can help minimize midnight trips to the outhouse. Just in case, before you bunk down, place a pair of sandals or camp shoes near your tent door. Put a patch of carpet or a camp towel outside the tent door to serve as a shoe-cleaning doormat. If you tend to get thirsty in the night, keep a water bottle next to your sleeping bag.

Campers are often amazed at how dark the night feels outdoors. It's a nice idea to hang a small LED lantern inside your tent as soon as you pitch it, so you can turn on a light when you prepare for bed. Fancy tents now come with built-in LED lights for a gentle glow. You will also need a good flashlight, or better yet, a battery-powered lantern. You might remember the old Coleman lanterns of our childhood and the comforting sound they made, but they burn white gas and make a flame. NO FLAME IS EVER ALLOWED IN A TENT. In the old days, tents were made of oiled cotton fabric. Now they are made of nylon and plastic, which melt when exposed to flame or even high heat. Remember to take the flashlight or lantern in the tent with you in case you have to go to the outhouse in the middle of the night.

Night noises. Some novice campers lie there listening anxiously to every little sound outside the tent. It's wonderful to hear an owl, not so wonderful to think you hear a bear. Remember that small critters can sound large at night, so try to relax. If you've put away your food properly, you should be fine. Use earplugs if night noises bother you. The sound of a rushing stream can lull you to sleep if you're lucky enough to have one nearby.

Staying warm in bed. On warm summer nights, you may not even need to zip up your sleeping bag. Often campers will just tuck their feet into the bag's foot box and drape the bag over themselves. If you expect warm nights, bring a sheet and/or a light blanket from home. That might be all you need. Staying warm when the temperature drops is quite another story. Eat a meal or light snack before bed. The process of digestion warms you internally, which generates the heat you need to sleep comfortably. Drink a warm, nonalcoholic beverage before hopping in the sack. (Alcohol dilates blood vessels, spurring heat loss.) Do a little exercise before finally plunking down and nodding off. Not too much or you might get sweaty and wide awake. Sit-ups in your sleeping bag are an easy way to heat both you and your bag. Remember to wear your long underwear and clean, dry socks. If your neck tends to get cold, wear a cozy neck gaiter. Wear a warm knit hat if you're cold when you first get in your bag. You can pull it off in the night if you get too warm. Cinch the sleeping bag hood around your head, even if you're wearing a hat. On below-freezing nights, you might only leave an opening large enough for your nose and mouth. Add a closed-cell foam pad beneath your regular sleeping pad for extra insulation. Put a warm water bottle close to the core of your body, since your core is your body's chief heat-generating zone.

Camping with your dog. When you talk about camping alone, you mean camping without other people. But if you own a dog, that animal is coming with you. Right? Camping with a dog just makes camping better. Its joy is a continual reminder to drink in the moment. However, you must recognize that there are regulations you must follow when camping with your dog and these regulations vary depending on your destination. As a rule of thumb, dogs are allowed anywhere cars can go, so developed campgrounds generally allow dogs. Many state and local parks also have trails available to canines and some feature dog-specific amenities in their parks. A number of states and counties have compiled dog-related information on their webpage to make it easier to pick a campsite that allows dogs. Go to the organization's homepage and search "dogs"—a guide may pop up.

If you plan to bring your dog, keep these things in mind:

(1) Your dog will be your constant companion while camping—all campgrounds forbid leaving your dog alone at camp and nearly all of them require that you keep your dog on a leash while in camp.

(2) You will be expected to pick up your dog's poop and dispose of it or take it with you when you leave the campground.

(3) You cannot let your dog sleep outside at night. Nearly all campgrounds require that your dog sleep either in your tent or in your car. There are wild animals outside at night and the last thing anyone wants is for your dog to get into a fight with a skunk or a coyote. Sleeping with you will keep your dog safe (and hopefully quiet).

(4) Add a bowl, water, and kibble for your dog to your camping checklist. If you plan to take your dog hiking, consider adding a dog pack so it can carry everything it needs.

(5) Bring out the dog's food only during meals. Leaving it out all the time invites wildlife into your camp. If your dog is a nibbler, use a bowl that closes on top and save leftovers in your car.

■ ■
■ ■

I rarely light a lantern when I sit around the campfire. I prefer the warm light of the fire itself. And if there's any moonlight, it gives plenty of light once my eyes adjust to the dark. Even if there's no moon, starlight alone is often bright enough. I love to read in bed, so I always take a lantern in the tent with me. Before I go to sleep, I make sure I know where my car keys, my shoes, and my cell phone are. Once I'm settled in the comfy bed, I prop up the lantern just right and read until I fall asleep. In my life at home, there's always an alarm clock. But when I'm camping, I can stay up as late as I want with a good book in a small cozy circle of light and sleep as late as I want in the morning. Come to think of it, though, the forest is full of noise in the morning. Birds and critters usually wake me up at first light.

Campground outhouses are disgusting, quite frankly. I often camp with my dog and I can't leave him unattended in the campground, so what to do with him while I'm in the outhouse? Take him in with me. Once I left him outside tied to the outhouse door and he pulled on the leash so hard that the door popped open and there he stood looking in at me along with a whole troop of boy scouts. So now I take him into the outhouse with me. There is something uncomfortable about sitting in a rustic smelly space with your dog watching you, but what else can you do?

My longest camping trip was supposed to be seven days. It was early spring and I was eager to check out some new campgrounds. The forecast was for nighttime temperatures in the upper 20s and daytime highs in the 60s—perfect weather for exploring. I ended up camping in snow for two nights and rain for the next two. I was wet, cold, and muddy. I could barely muster the motivation to clean up and change clothes after reading in my tent for a solid eight hours, listening to the rain pour down. Every joint in my body was aching for a hot shower, so I tossed my gear in the car and headed toward town. I had my dog with me as always and wasn't confident that I could find a motel that accepted dogs.

I was turned down twice in one little town, then drove to the next little town and stopped at a run-down motel beside the highway. I walked inside to find a wom-

an and a couple of men sitting around a wood stove. They gave me the usual 'look what the cat dragged in' stares when I asked about a room. The woman told me the motel wasn't open yet; it was too early in the spring. Then I guess she took pity on me because she said she'd give me and my dog a room for the night. I handed her the cash and dragged my damp baggage in from the car. I closed the door, pulled the drapes, and cranked up the room heater on the wall. My dog promptly lay down in front of the heater and fell asleep. I turned on the shower and waited a few minutes, but got only cold water, so I turned it off and walked back to the motel lobby and asked the woman if there was any hot water. She told me that the hot water hadn't been turned on all winter and it would take a little while for the tank to heat up. She invited me to sit awhile in front of her fire. We got to talking and she was astonished to hear that I'd been outside for the past five days. She asked me why I'd camp in such a remote area when the weather is so terrible. I replied that I just had to get away from the city and then we got to talking about fishing. She invited me to her house behind the hotel for dinner. Best meatloaf I've ever eaten.

■ ■
■ ■

Staying Safe

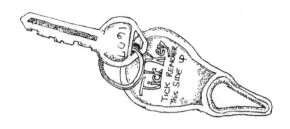

What keeps you awake at night when you go camping? Getting mauled by a bear? In reality, that's extremely unlikely. According to the U.S. National Park Service, during the six years between 2007 and 2013, the Number 1 cause of death in national parks wasn't wildlife attacks; it was drowning (365 deaths, mostly boating, kayaking, and rafting accidents). The Number 2 cause of death was traffic accidents (210 deaths, 42 of them were people on motorcycles). The Number 3 cause of death was falls (178 deaths, mostly while hiking). Way down the list was wildlife attacks. Four people died from attacks by grizzly bears and one person died from an attack by a crazed mountain goat. One other person died from a snakebite. These statistics say that wildlife attacks should be your least worry. Yes, there are big animals out there with sharp fangs, claws, horns, and hooves, but they just want to be left alone and will almost never attack you unless you corner them (or their babies). You should be more worried about certain bugs and plants.

Ticks are dark brown arachnids about the size of sesame seeds. They live in bushes and grass and jump onto you as you walk by. Then they crawl around on your clothing looking for an opening. If they find one, they burrow their heads into your skin and drink your blood. If you are bitten by a tick, you probably won't even notice it. You have to check your body for tiny dark lumps. If you find one and you can easily brush it off, then it hasn't bitten you yet and that's a relief. If you do find one embedded in your skin, it has already bitten you, but don't panic. Don't try to scrape it off or burn it or pinch it or tweeze it out. Trying to remove a tick by any of these methods will squish it, leaving its head embedded in your skin. It's better to remove it using tick key. (Always carry one of these on your key chain when camping.)

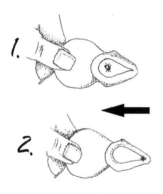

You press the tick key against your skin with the tick in the tear-drop hole. Then you slide the tick key across your skin so the tick ends up in the narrow tapered slot and then slowly pull the tick key away from your skin. The tick comes out, head and all. Afterwards you should put some antibacterial medicine or alcohol on the tick key and on the spot on your skin where the tick was.

Some ticks are infected with serious diseases, such as Lyme disease or Rocky Mountain spotted fever, and can transmit these diseases when they bite you. The earliest evidence of Lyme disease is a skin rash near the bite. This occurs about a week after the bite. The rash expands into a reddish splotch that looks like a bull's eye—a center red dot with a distinct red ring around the center. Rocky Mountain spotted fever's initial symptoms are high fever, headache, chills, muscle pain, and deep fatigue. A few days later, a spotted rash appears first on the hands and feet and then elsewhere. This characteristic rash gives Rocky Mountain spotted fever its name. If you notice any of these signs or symptoms, see a doctor immediately.

The best way to avoid tick bites is to keep them off your body. Insect repellents that contain DEET at levels of 20-30% are effective. Don't hesitate to douse your shoes, boots, and pants cuffs. Picardin is another repellent you can use directly on your skin. Permethrin also repels ticks, but it can only be used on your clothing, not on your skin.

 Mosquitoes and other biting insects. Mosquitoes find you by detecting the carbon dioxide in your breath and the chemicals in your sweat. The female mosquito is the one that bites. She has a mouthpart designed to pierce skin and siphon off blood. As she fills herself with blood, she injects saliva into your skin and proteins in her saliva trigger an immune reaction that causes the characteristic itching and bump. The bump usually clears up on its own in a few days, but some people get a large area of swelling, soreness, and redness (sometimes referred to as "skeeter syndrome").

Occasionally a mosquito bite leads to more serious signs— fever, headache, body aches, and signs of infection. If that happens, contact your doctor. Mosquitoes can carry diseases, such as West Nile virus, malaria, yellow fever, and dengue fever. A mosquito gets the virus or parasite by biting an infected person or animal and then when it bites you, transfers that virus or parasite through its saliva. West Nile and encephalitis viruses are found in the United States. Dengue fever has been reported in several southern states and Hawaii. Other diseases, such as malaria and yellow fever, are far more common in tropical countries.

To protect yourself from mosquito bites, use insect repellent. The most effective insect repellents in the United States contain one of three active ingredients—DEET, picaridin, or oil of lemon eucalyptus. These repellents temporarily repel mosquitoes and ticks. Whichever product you choose, read the label before you apply it. If you're using a spray repellent, apply it outdoors and away from food. Don't apply repellent under clothing. Don't apply repellent over sunburns, cuts, wounds or rashes. When you get back home, wash with soap and water to remove any remaining repellent.

For additional protection, you can use Permethrin, an insecticide and insect repellent that you apply to clothing and outdoor gear, not skin. Weather permitting, you can also protect yourself by wearing long-sleeved shirts, socks and closed-toe shoes, long pants (better yet, tuck them into the tops of your socks and wrap with duct tape), light colors, and a hat that protects your ears and neck or one with mosquito netting that covers your head.

Chiggers attach themselves to your hair follicles. These pests grab onto your clothing as you hike in brushy areas, crawl around until they find bare skin, and can feed upon you for several days. The saliva from their bite can cause an allergic response. Fire ants are common in the southern United States, especially in sandy areas. They give painful bites that feel like you're suddenly on fire. Black flies (also known as gnats in many areas) resemble small houseflies. Their bites are usually painless because they first inject a natural anesthetic and then suck or sponge up your blood. Black flies are most active in the late afternoon and evening. They prefer warm, humid weather and dislike cool, dry breezes. The peak season is late spring and early summer. Bug repellents such as DEET are not as effective for black flies as they are for mosquitoes and ticks, so protection must come from proper clothing and netting. Horseflies and deerflies are larger and noisier than blackflies. Repellents don't work. About all you can do is cover up with clothing and be fast on the swat.

Bees - Thick Waist

Wasps, bees, and hornets try to avoid you, but if you bother them or stumble onto one of their nests, they will sting. Wasps may sting without provocation. They are often found around garbage cans and food. Wasps are shiny and smooth with a thin waist.

Bees are much less likely to sting and will also go to great lengths to avoid you. Bees also have a fuzzy appearance and a thick waist; they are easy to identify. Bees are often near flowers, not your campsite.

Most of the time, these stings cause only minor signs and symptoms—sharp burning pain, redness, and slight swelling at the sting site, which go away within a few hours. Some people have stronger reactions—extreme swelling and redness at the sting site that gradually enlarges over the next day or two and takes five to ten days to go away. If you have strong reactions when you get stung, talk to your doctor about it, especially if your reactions are becoming more severe each time. There's a significant chance you could develop anaphylaxis the next time you get stung. The signs and symptoms of anaphylaxis include hives and itching, flushed or pale skin, difficulty breathing, swelling of the throat and tongue, a weak, rapid pulse, nausea, vomiting or diarrhea, and loss of consciousness. Anaphylaxis is potentially life-threatening and requires emergency treatment, even if it's just one or two signs or symptoms. If you were prescribed an emergency epinephrine auto injector (such as Epipen or Auvi-Q), use it right away. Call 911.

Scorpions are found mainly in desert regions of southern California, Arizona, New Mexico, Texas and Northern Mexico. They like to hide underneath rocks, wood, and leaves and may wander into your shoes, clothing, or sleeping bag. Healthy adults rarely need treatment for scorpion stings. Signs and symptoms are usually localized—pain (which can be intense), numbness, tingling, and swelling in the area around the sting. Occasionally symptoms are more severe—difficulty breathing, muscle twitching, sweating, nausea, and vomiting. If you begin to experience severe symptoms, seek prompt medical care. A person who has previously been stung by scorpions may develop an allergic reaction severe enough to cause anaphylaxis. Signs and symptoms in these cases are similar to those of anaphylaxis caused by bee stings and can include hives, trouble breathing, nausea, and vomiting.

Poison Ivy/Poison Sumac/Poison Oak:
All of these plants can cause misery. They share the same oleoresin called *urushiol*—a sticky, clear oil that exudes from the plant's leaves, stems, and roots. This substance is present in live and dead plants and even in the smoke when they are burned. It causes contact dermatitis—an itchy, blistering rash— if you touch the plant or even an object, such as clothing, that has touched the plant. Once you touch urushiol, it takes about ten to fifteen minutes for the rash to appear. First it looks like a mosquito bite and then it develops into an itchy rash. The itchy area enlarges in size to become a large, reddened, raised, and blistered area and it may spread as the toxic oil moves to adjacent skin areas. If you know you've touched a plant, immediately try to remove the toxin. You have ten to fifteen minutes to do so. Rinse thoroughly with cold water. Warm water will open your pores and make things worse. A solvent, such as alcohol, poured over the area first and then rinsed with copious amounts of cold water is also effective. Hydrogen peroxide or bleach added to the cold water also helps. Symptoms usually take about a week to clear up. It's important to take off contaminated clothing, place it in a plastic bag, and take it straight to the washing machine.

The best defense is avoidance. Remember the saying, "Leaves of three, let them be." Poison ivy has smooth-edged leaves while poison oak has serrated or lobed leaves. Poison sumac has a different leaf pattern. It is found in marshy areas, so it's not a big problem for

campers, but poison ivy and oak can grow just about anywhere where the elevation is below 5000 to 6000 feet. It's in
the creek bottoms and slopes where hiking trails are common.

Bears and other critters. When you go
camping, you are sharing space with
wild animals. It's always a thrill when
you spot one of them, but it's better if
they're not too close. Especially bears.
There are two species of bears that live
where you are likely to camp. Black
bears and brown (or grizzly) bears. (There are polar bears,
too, but they live mostly above the Arctic Circle and you
probably won't be camping up there.)

Black bears are common in sparse-
ly settled, forested areas across
most of the northern United
States and Canada. Your chance
of being attacked by a black bear
is virtually zero. Still worried?
Take along some bear spray (also
called pepper spray) and an air
horn. It's true that black bears
tend to hang around camp-
grounds; they're looking for food. Never leave food out at
your campsite when you go to bed or leave for the day. Never.
And that goes for dirty dishes, deodorant, toothpaste, or anything else that smells like food. Store all that stuff in your car.
Food left outside attracts not only bears, but also raccoons,
opossums, chipmunks, and various other critters that will
come into your camp and toss everything to get a morsel.

Grizzly bears live in Alaska, northern and western Canada, and portions of the Rocky Mountains in the United States. If you are camping in grizzly country, be really careful—they're huge and powerful and have been known to attack people for no reason. If a grizzly approaches, you will be tempted to run for your life, but the experts say that's not a good idea. They say to avoid eye contact and walk away slowly. If the bear charges, stand your ground (you can't outrun a grizzly). Don't scream or yell. Speak in a soft monotone voice and wave your arms to let the animal know you are human. If the animal gets real close and you have pepper spray, use it. If the animal makes contact, curl up into a ball on your side or lie flat on your stomach, and remain as quiet as possible until the attack ends. Yowsers!

Mountain lions are widespread in the U.S. and Canada. They can hear and smell you miles away and really want nothing to do with you. They won't come into your camp. If you should ever spot one on the trail, consider yourself lucky, as they are a rare sight. Same with wolves. They were once hunted nearly to extinction, but now they're protected and making a comeback. They're also extremely shy, so it's unlikely that you'll ever see one.

Bad weather: Check your local weather before you leave and if severe weather is in the forecast, think about rescheduling your trip. In the Midwest, severe weather means rain and thunderstorms, sudden snowstorms, or extreme heat. If you find yourself in a situation where your tent is flooding, tornadoes are in the area, or the temperatures plummet, pack up and check into a motel. There's no shame in that.

 **Bad water.** You should take drinking water with you. If you run out of water or cannot carry enough water with you for your entire trip, you may be tempted to obtain drinking water from natural water sources. Drinking untreated water such as bore water, river water, or spring water (including mineral springs) can lead to illnesses such as gastroenteritis and diarrhea.

Men. Sometimes I am asked, "Aren't you afraid of being accosted while camping alone?" and I answer, "No, I'm not." When people say that women camping alone are reckless, they really don't understand the realities of sexual assault. Women are most likely to be assaulted in their own homes and more than three-quarters of them know their attackers. Statistically, you're safer camping alone than you are letting your creepy ex into your house. You will certainly encounter drunks in campgrounds. They play loud music and drink beer from cans and invariably one of them falls into the campfire, but generally they are harmless. If one of these guys wanders over to your campsite and tries to strike up a conversation, politely tell him you appreciate his offer of a beer, but are really looking for some quiet time alone. He'll wander back to rejoin his buddies.

That said, it doesn't hurt to be careful. Tell trusted family or friends where you'll be camping and when you plan to return and ask them to notify the authorities if you don't return when expected. Don't advertise the fact that you're camping alone when you go to get water or ice in a nearby town. Be mindful of who is camping around you. If you stumble onto a guy who really creeps you out, don't hesitate to pack up and go to another campsite. I have loaded up my gear and left in the dark a couple of times. You can't count on having cell phone reception while camping, but if things get weird, call 911 anyway. You may be able to get through.

Bigfoot. Over the years, there have been numerous sightings of hairy, ape-like bipeds that stand seven to nine feet tall and weigh between 600 and 900 pounds. These creatures are covered with long brown or black hair about an inch long and they possess extraordinary strength. They mostly inhabit remote mountainous regions of the Pacific Northwest and western Canada, where they are called "Sasquatch." Bigfoot tends to avoid humans and sightings are extremely rare. If you spot one, take a picture and send it to me.

Just kidding.

Getting lost. When you go hiking, the best way to avoid getting lost is to stay on the trail, but let's say you ignore my advice and wander off into the woods, lost in thought, admiring the flowers and trees. Time passes. Suddenly, you don't recognize your surroundings and can't tell the direction you came from. You're lost.

Once you realize you're lost, you're going to panic. Everyone does. You know this is going to happen, so resist the temptation to go tearing off through the underbrush. Tell yourself to sit still until you calm down and are able to think clearly again. Then try to retrace your steps back to the trail.

If that doesn't work, then you are truly lost and unlikely to find your way back to your campsite, so you'll just have to settle for getting to somewhere there's people. If possible, move to higher ground to give yourself a better chance of seeing a river, lake, road, or church steeple that can help you orient yourself. Pick a direction in which to walk, but carefully mark your progress with rocks, cairns, or piles of sticks so you go in a straight line and don't end up walking in a circle. Periodically scan your surroundings for any sign of human activity—old campsites, cut tree stumps, fishing line, food wrappers, cigarette butts, plastic water bottles. If you find any such evidence, look around to see if you can to determine which way the people went—you may be near a trail or road that can lead you out or a logging or hunting camp that can provide emergency shelter.

Every once in a while, stop crunching through the leaves and listen. The sound of a well-traveled road or church bell can be heard a fair distance away, even through dense forest. Your best choice of direction is almost always downhill. People tend to settle in valleys, usually close to water. Unless you have seen signs of people at higher elevations, head downhill. Besides, you can cover more terrain and conserve energy traveling downhill. If you come across a stream or river, follow it in the direction the water is running. Water flowing downhill can lead you to a town or populated lake—and you'll have a source of emergency drinking water. If the stream is moving slowly, drop a few leaves into the water to determine the direction of the current. If darkness settles in, it's a good idea to stay put and start walking again at sunrise. If all else fails, call 911.

Getting hurt. There are many sharp and hot things in your campsite and plenty of places to stumble and fall on the trail, so you're bound to get your share of burns, bruises, scrapes, and sprains. Count on it. If your injuries are minor, you can treat them yourself using the medical kit that you should bring to your campsite and always carry with you when you go hiking. If you get badly hurt and don't think you can make it to a medical facility by yourself, the first thing you should do is call for help from neighboring campers or passers-by on the trail. If there's nobody around, call 911.

A note about calling 911. Before you leave on a camping trip, be sure to leave your cell phone number and the name of your wireless service provider with trusted family or friends. Also let them know when you expect to return and ask them to notify the authorities if you don't show up. Always keep your cell phone with you in camp and on the trail. If you get hopelessly lost or badly injured, dial 911 even if you have no signal. Even without cell service, attempting to dial 911 or even turning on your phone intermittently could transmit an electronic signal that lets rescuers know you need help. If possible, head for higher ground to get a stronger signal—cell phones operate by line-of-sight radio waves.

Here's how it works. Calling 911 on a cell phone connects you to the nearest PSAP (public safety answering point). Before the 911 operator can ask "What's your emergency?" a computer has already triangulated your latitude and longitude coordinates to within a few hundred feet using signal telemetry, your phone's GPS chip, or both. Even if your 911 call doesn't go through, your wireless provider may still have a record of your position and the exact time you tried to make the call. Your cell phone and the nearest tower constantly talk to each other—something called digital "handshaking."

Unlike voice calls or text messages, these electronic packets require very little energy to send or receive. Sometimes they take place even when your phone indicates no reception. Sometimes they bounce off towers that your phone doesn't have permission to use. And sometimes they get through when they shouldn't—like in remote and mountainous terrain. In almost all cases, this data trail is logged and saved on the computer of your service provider. If you go missing, your family or friends can give your phone number and service provider's name to law enforcement officials. They can then call your service provider's special emergency hotline and access the data trail for your phone.

Be careful out there.

■ ■
■ ■

I camped once at a rustic, but popular campground in the fall. The man camping next to me was camping alone with his dog and he seemed harmless. Our two dogs met and we exchanged pleasantries and went about our respective businesses. At 1 a.m., I awoke to find more cars and people talking at his site. I listened for a little bit and heard them say they were going to harvest the marijuana they'd grown on the property next door. I stayed quiet as they took off down the trail and when they came back at 4 a.m. They stayed up the rest of the night drinking beer. I was up and out of there before sunrise.

I was camping alone a few miles from the river and drove to what looked like a promising fishing spot. I parked my car near a washed-out bridge and was get-

ting my fishing stuff out when an older man stepped out of a white pickup truck with a set of long-horn steer horns across the front and asked me what a pretty thing like me was doing all alone beside the road. I told him I was going fishing. He said that he lived just up the road and I should stop by for a cup of coffee or a beer. I had no intention of doing that, but when I was finished fishing and driving back up the road, there he was gesturing for me to stop. Against my better judgment, I did stop and now I am glad I did. He was a perfectly nice gentleman who made a good cup of coffee. He showed me around his place and pointed out a couple of cabins where he said I could stay any time. The following year, I was driving down the same road headed for the same fishing spot and guess who was standing beside the road.

I ended up staying in one of his little cabins. I was nervous at first, but he showed to a cabin with a real bed and everything and handed me a shotgun, warning me that it was loaded and the safety did not work. I asked him why he was handing me a shotgun and he told me it was in case I thought he meant me harm. I set the gun behind the door and as far as I know, it's still there. The next day I went fishing, then we had dinner on the grill and talked and in the morning, we had breakfast at the local diner. I always stop by to see him when I'm in the area.

I was camping with a friend in a remote area and I went to bed, but she stayed up, ate some crackers, and left the package open on the picnic table. Around 3 a.m., we were awakened by a loud crash. We listened for a few minutes and heard cellophane rustling and some-

thing snuffling. Bear! I picked up my flashlight, zipped open the tent, and trained the light on the table. There were cracker crumbs everywhere and a flipped-over camp stove and a propane canister on the ground. A large fat raccoon rose up from behind the campfire ring clutching the package of crackers. He laid back his ears and hissed at me and when I moved toward him, he snatched the package in his teeth and scurried off into the bushes, cracker package bumping along behind him.

I only met a bear face-to-face one time. I was wading calf-deep in a small river fishing for trout. I couldn't hear anything over the sound of the rushing water, so I didn't heard it approach. I caught a movement in the corner of my eye and looked up and there was a black bear, maybe 30 feet away on the riverbank. I stumbled back a step and the bear stumbled back a step, clearly as surprised as I was, and then it turned around and crashed into the underbrush. That's it, that's my bear story.

∷

Summary

As I hope you have seen, camping alone isn't hard to do. You can go whenever you want—for a night, two nights, a week. You'll need to buy some basic equipment—a book of maps, a tent, and a sleeping bag to start, and a few other comfort and safety items.

What you can't buy is the experience. The experience is free and yours to create. I have spent whole days in camp writing in my journal, hunched over a picnic table. I have spent whole days tramping on trails and driving on two-tracks. I have spent whole days sitting beside a lake reading a book or just doing nothing under a canopy of fall leaves. If you're like me, you'll start out being not so sure camping is for you, but you'll spend night or two in a tent and learn to read a map. You'll become a little more enthusiastic and confident the next time you go camping and even more the time after that. You'll end up seeking new destinations and new activities you never knew were there.

:·:

Camping Gear Checklist

This is a complete list of everything mentioned in this book. You may not need every item for every camping trip.

Getting there:

- ☐ *Gas in vehicle*
- ☐ *ID*
- ☐ *Credit cards*
- ☐ *Money*
- ☐ *Reservations and permits*
- ☐ *Atlas and gazetteer*
- ☐ *GPS*
- ☐ *Cell phone*
- ☐ *Glasses*

Shelter:

- ☐ *Tent*
- ☐ *Tent poles*
- ☐ *Tent stakes*
- ☐ *Tarp*
- ☐ *Tent patching kit*

Sleeping:

- ☐ *Sleeping bag*
- ☐ *Sleeping pad*
- ☐ *Air pump*
- ☐ *Air pump batteries*

- [ ] *Sleeping pad patching kit*
- [ ] *Blankets*
- [ ] *Pillow*
- [ ] *Flashlight*
- [ ] *Lantern*
- [ ] *Flashlight and lantern batteries*

Clothing:

- [ ] *Hiking boots*
- [ ] *Camp shoes*
- [ ] *Molefoam padding*
- [ ] *Inner socks*
- [ ] *Outer socks*
- [ ] *Underwear*
- [ ] *Pants*
- [ ] *Shirts*
- [ ] *Shorts*
- [ ] *Sweatshirt/hoodie/sweater*
- [ ] *Coat*
- [ ] *Raincoat*
- [ ] *Wool hat*
- [ ] *Baseball cap*
- [ ] *Swimsuit*
- [ ] *Bandana*
- [ ] *Gloves*

Hygiene:

- [ ] *Toilet paper*

- ☐ *Toothbrush and toothpaste*
- ☐ *Deodorant*
- ☐ *Face wipes*
- ☐ *Brush/comb*

Campfire:

- ☐ *Firewood*
- ☐ *Kindling*
- ☐ *Tinder*
- ☐ *Axe*
- ☐ *Lighter and/or matches*
- ☐ *Flint and steel set*

Cooking:

- ☐ *Food*
- ☐ *Cooler*
- ☐ *Ice*
- ☐ *Drinking water*
- ☐ *Campfire grill*
- ☐ *Camp stove*
- ☐ *Propane canisters*
- ☐ *Aluminum foil*
- ☐ *Dish Soap*
- ☐ *Bleach and water mix*
- ☐ *Paper towels*
- ☐ *Cleaning rags*
- ☐ *Cooking utensils*
- ☐ *Oven mitt*

- ☐ *Plates and bowls*
- ☐ *Zip-lock bags*
- ☐ *Garbage bags*

Safety*:*

- ☐ *Tick key*
- ☐ *Insect repellant*
- ☐ *Whistle or air horn*
- ☐ *Pepper spray*
- ☐ *First aid kit*

98687523R00059

Made in the USA
Columbia, SC
30 June 2018